Meditation

The All In One Guide To Cleansing, Fasting, And Meditation That Will Help Your Body Heal Itself And Look Better Than Ever

(The Definitive Meditation Instruction Manual For Newcomers)

Ravinder Hyde

TABLE OF CONTENT

What Is Meditation? 1

What Is Stress? 6

Why Should You Begin To Meditate Right Now!? 16

The 7 Chakras 28

Put Obstacles In Front Of Yourself 38

The Meditations That Only Take Five Minutes 42

The Mental Process And Ideas 51

Positive Meditation May Help Improve Both Your Spiritual And Emotional Outlook On Life. Here Are Some Of The Secrets To Doing So. 58

Meditation With A Guided For The Purification Of The Mind 62

Meditations With A Guided Focus On Happiness 71

The Composition Of The Elements Within The Human Hand And Mudras 80

Insolvent, Bitter, And Shattered To The Core . 84

What Is The Shakti Of The Kundalini? 88

Alternative Methods Of Meditation 93

- Alterations Made To The Brain 100
- Remarquements And Acknowledgements 104
- Try One Of These Ten Varieties Of Meditation 111
- The Actual Process Of Meditating 116
- Practising Mindfulness Each And Every Day 126
- A General Explanation Of Meditation 132
- When You Are Under Pressure, What Can You Expect To Happen? 144
- Problems That Frequently Affect Children's Sleep 154
- An Explanation Of The Chakras 166

What Is Meditation?

Zen Buddhism places a strong emphasis on meditation as a central practise. The practise of meditation consists of doing nothing at all. The majority of people are of the opinion that practising meditation is the activity that is most beneficial to one's growth as a person. It is possible that it would be more accurate to argue that the most effective approach to grow as a person is to engage in absolutely no activity at all. The profound paradox of meditation is that its practise consists of doing nothing at all. You live your life, you pay attention to the way you breathe, and finally you reach a point where you can just appreciate living and breathing on their own without needing anything else. And eventually, when you have achieved a high level of mastery in doing nothing, you will understand that there is nothing more for you to do. Another one of life's ironies is that just when you think you have nothing to do, you realise that you really become extremely adept at doing things. This is but one example of the inherent contradictions that may be found in Zen. According to the words of the philosopher Krishnatmurti, "You have nothing to do. Now go out and do something. People are preoccupied with doing things in the hope that they will get better or progress in some manner, but in reality all that is required of them is to do nothing at all.

Many people believe that meditation consists of sitting still for long periods of time, focusing on nothing in particular, while being totally at ease and untroubled. And many experienced meditators can attest to this being the case. But this is not the case for most people. One may argue that there is a scale, and at one end of the scale is meditation, calm, and oneness, while at the other end is tension, worry, overload, and anxiety. People who spend an unhealthy amount of time on the extremes of the scale have a greater need to practise meditation. On the other hand, there are certain individuals who are always operating in a condition that is more analogous to meditation. If you do find that meditation is difficult for you, then you should try to find another activity that is soothing and, in some way, puts your mind at ease. This might take the form of a stroll in the great outdoors, Chi Gong, or Yoga. It is important to keep in mind that Zen does not care how you get to it and that each person is unique. Finding their Zen may require some individuals to shut their eyes and meditate for sixty minutes. Others may discover Zen via the act of gardening.

The activity that allows me to feel the most at ease is cruising slowly through the forest on a scooter. There is no set path that one must follow in order to achieve Zen, just as there is no set path that one must follow in order to achieve enlightenment. However, despite the fact that this is the case, meditation remains the method that has been around the longest and can be used in any context. Because of this, it is recommended that one give meditation at least one month's worth of effort before delving into other Zen practises.

The key to successful meditation is to achieve a state in which the mind is calm and still. A Zen state may finally be achieved by maintaining mental stillness and passivity for an extended period of time. Observe the skilled movements of a yogi or a Tai Chi practitioner. These are moving meditations, in which the mind is at rest while the body moves more or less unconsciously and in a predetermined pattern. The best way to improve is to practise. There are two primary types of meditation, namely sitting still and practising mindfulness, along with walking meditation.

In its most basic form, meditation is nothing more than an extended period of calm. We have all encountered folks who seem unaffected by the trials and tribulations of everyday life. They are able to do it on autopilot. On the other hand, some of us have allowed ourselves to get entangled in a web of stress and commitments, and as a result, life has become more of a chore than a delight. Simply practising meditation and letting go of these things will allow us to be fully present in the here and now and have pleasure in life.

What Is Stress?

The majority of people will experience some level of stress at some point in their lives. The emotional reaction that humans have to pressure is referred to as stress. The effects of stress on certain individuals might become so overpowering that it is difficult for them to cope with it. The situation of being stressed may sometimes grow so severe that it causes people to have physical difficulties. When it comes to these particular people, tension may become so severe that it is difficult to manage. There is no doubt that stress can completely take over a person's life. Because of the increased risk of health issues that might emerge as a direct consequence of stress, stress is sometimes referred to as "the silent killer." It is believed that stress might cause the two disorders that are the most likely to result in death: cancer and heart disease. It is vital that you take action as soon as possible if you have discovered yourself to be under the utmost amount of stress. The longer you are under stress, the greater the number and severity of the risks that it exposes you to.

The following are some of the potential dangers of stress:

Lack of sleep

Lack of capacity to focus or concentrate

Easily irritated

Having constant feelings of exhaustion and fatigue

Pain in the head

Unease in the Stomach

Having trouble with one's breathing

Pain in the Chest and Shaking

Stress, if left untreated, may lead to a variety of health concerns, including heart disease, issues with mental health, and a host of other issues. People who are under a lot of pressure often get the impression that they are going insane or that they are unable to cope with the mental components of their situation and are losing their minds.

The Risk Factors of Stress

An individual's level of stress may be caused by a variety of external causes. These are the following:

Concerns pertaining to one's place of employment Difficulties in one's personal relationships, whether they with one's partner, children, or other members of one's family

The passing of a family member

preparing to enter wedlock

Purchasing a House Giving a Presentation to a Group In open view

These are only some of the numerous factors that might put us in a stressful situation. There are many more. It's possible that anything that stresses one individual out won't do the same to another. Because everyone of us is unique, it is essential for you to get an understanding of how to recognise the sources of stress in your own life. It is also essential to keep in mind that the method in which you deal with stress may be affected not only by your career but also by your family history and personality.

When you are under a lot of pressure, what happens?

When a person is stressed, their heart rate speeds up, they become more tensein their muscles, they breathe more quickly, and the volume of blood that flows to their muscles and brain may rise by as much as 400%. When you are under a lot of stress on a consistent basis, not only is your physical health at risk, but so is your mental and emotional wellbeing.

When you're under a lot of pressure, your body reacts by giving you headaches, back pain, stomach difficulties, weariness, and a whole host of other symptoms that you're definitely going to be able to feel. Stress is causing numerous changes to take place behind the scenes, and these changes are also occuring. Stress may have an effect on the white blood cells in your body that help you fight infections. It can also raise the risk of stress and heart attacks, and it can lead to risky behaviours such as smoking, drug use, and alcohol use. Your sexual health may also be significantly impacted by stress. When you are under a lot of pressure, the thought of having sex is usually the last thing from your mind. The fact that it is more difficult to have an orgasm when you are stressed is another factor that adds to the pessimistic attitude on sexual encounters.

It is very necessary for you to figure out how to exercise control over the sources of stress in your life if you want to lead a lifestyle that is healthy and emotionally stable. You need to be able to recognise the signs of stress as they appear, and you also need to be able to acquire coping mechanisms that will assist you in feeling less overwhelmed.

How to Get Rid of Your Stress

If you are reading this book, you are either at the end of your rope with stress or you want to get right down to business and put an end to stress before it has a chance to interfere with your life. Getting rid of stress in your life may be accomplished in a variety of different methods, some of which we have already discussed. The most effective approach is often one that makes use of a number of these various techniques and approaches concurrently. On the other hand, you may also try meditating in order to put an end to the problem once and for all.

You should discuss the possibility of taking anti-anxiety medication with your primary care physician. These drugs may provide short-term relief from the symptoms of worry and stress. There is a wide variety of drugs available that may assist in the reduction or removal of stress. Medication is something that should only be taken for short-term periods of time, and it is not always the best option for every person. There is a possibility of becoming addicted to some anti-anxiety drugs, so this is something else that should be taken into account.

In addition to taking medication, you could also find that participating in psychotherapy might be of aid to you in working through the issues that are causing you to feel stressed. It is always comforting to have someone there with whom you can chat and who is willing to listen to what you are experiencing and how you are feeling. Talking to a therapist is beneficial for a number of reasons, one of which is the opportunity to get helpful guidance and pointers for managing stress. However, at the end of the day, there is only so much that can be accomplished for you by talking to another person. To alleviate the stress in your life, it is still up to you to take the required actions and get your life in order.

Meditation, on the other hand, is without a doubt the most effective strategy for removing stress from one's life. When you meditate, you are doing a lot more than only momentarily restraining the tension that is buried deep within of you. You are removing it from your life, as well as your head and the ideas that you have. You are breaking free of your shackles. Meditation is completely safe to practise; there are no possible negative consequences, no fears, and no hazards linked with doing so. People who use meditation to alleviate stress discover that it not only helps them reduce the amount of stress they are now feeling but also helps them better manage and reduce the amount of stress they will experience in the future.

The practise of altering the way you think by gradually transitioning into a different mental state via the use of your thinking process is what is known as meditation. When you alter the way that you think, your whole mental state changes, and with that shift comes a rapid disappearance of stress and the symptoms associated with it.

Why Should You Begin To Meditate Right Now!?

These days, a lot of people are getting into meditation. among point of fact, it's become something of a catchphrase among the "new age" community. Because these practises have been widely covered in numerous publications, blogs, and well-known talk programmes like Oprah, an increasing number of individuals are beginning to meditate and practise yoga. Jennifer Aniston, Paula Abdul, Kristen Bell, Sheryl Crow, Jim Carrey, Ellen DeGeneres, Mia Farrow, Jane Fonda, Hugh Jackman, Nicole Kidman, Naomi Watts, Miranda Kerr, and Madonna are just few of the famous people that meditate on a daily basis. Others who meditate include Paula Abdul, Kristen Bell, Sheryl Crow, Jim Carrey, and Ellen DeGeneres.

The capacity of meditation to induce both physical and mental relaxation has contributed to the practice's widespread popularity. In this day and age, when everyone seems to be overworked and exhausted, we want something that might help us become more rooted. We need something that will shield us from all of the worry, pressure, and stress that we are now under.

The following is a list of the most persuasive arguments in favour of beginning meditation right away:

Increased Capacity for Concentration – Mind deterioration is often brought on by factors such as stress, strain, and the natural process of ageing. Because of these things, you will often struggle with your cognitive abilities as well as other functions of your brain, which will make it tough for you to concentrate and focus on what you're doing. You might think of meditation as a mental practise or a type of mental training that will improve your ability to concentrate and focus on what you're doing. If you meditate on a daily basis, you will find that it is much simpler for you to focus on highly essential work, such as studying or writing. If you meditate on a daily basis, you won't let things like the internet or social networking sites pull your attention away from your practise.

Because meditation is a practise for relaxation, it helps to enhance the immune system, which in turn leads to improved immunological function. Meditation not only strengthens the body's defences against a wide range of illnesses, but it also assists the body in its battle against cancer cells and viruses. If you have seen that your health has been worsening and that you are now more prone to getting the flu and a fever, then you should begin meditating as soon as possible before it is too late to do so.

Increased Fertility - Research has shown that women who meditate on a regular basis have increased fertility compared to those who do not meditate. A higher sperm count is generally associated with males who meditate, according to the findings of one research.

Regular Meditation Practitioners Have Lower Blood Pressure According to a Study Conducted at the Harvard Medical School, those who meditate on a regular basis have lower blood pressure. If you reduce your blood pressure, your body is less likely to respond to the hormones that are produced in response to stress.

tension and anxiety may be alleviated by meditation - It is well established that meditation can soothe tension and anxiety. If you are continually put in stressful situations, whether via work, relationships, or circumstances, it is in your best interest to meditate on a regular basis.

Tranquilly Meditation has a calming effect on the nervous system, and it also helps practitioners become more relaxed. Meditation enables you to maintain your composure even when confronted with emotionally trying scenarios and circumstances.

Emotional steadiness is a benefit that may accrue to meditators as they learn to become more centred and in charge of their own feelings. The expression of emotions might at times be unpredictable. Emotions have the ability to ensnare you and give you the impression that you are riding a roller coaster, complete with regular twists and turns, as well as ups and downs. You may get rid of all the negative thoughts in your head by practising meditation. It has the potential to assist you in overcoming emotional baggage. Additionally, it might assist you in achieving mental clarity and calmness.

Improved creative output is a potential benefit of practising some types of meditation, particularly those that are geared at reawakening the Kundalini energy. People who regularly engage in more advanced forms of meditation often report experiencing an unprompted outpouring of creative thoughts. People who meditate on a regular basis have a greater capacity for creativity and the arts. Steve Jobs, who was a practitioner of meditation, attributes his revitalised creativity when he established Pixar to his spiritual practise. Jobs was a practitioner of meditation.

People who meditate on a daily basis are less susceptible to the attacks of naysayers and naysaying organisations because meditation strengthens their immune systems. They have a lower propensity to take things personally to an excessive degree. Practitioners of meditation have the ability to quiet the voice of their inner critic and embrace oneself more fully.

If you are already in your early thirties or forties and you still have not figured out what you want to accomplish with your life, then it is time for you to start meditating. Meditation helps you find your true north. Meditation puts you in touch with who you really are and why you're here. Meditation puts you in touch with what it is you really want out of life and helps you become more aware of those desires.

Intuition may be improved by meditation because it gives clarity, and this in turn increases your intuition, which acts as your inner guide. Meditation may help you get a deeper understanding of who you are. Through meditation, you may bring your mind, body, and spirit into harmony with the divine as well as with those of other people. You are going to experience certain epiphanies in which you will get superior information. In spite of the masks that others put on, it will be much simpler for you to arrive at the correct conclusions and recognise the genuine character of other individuals.

You may become closer to the holy via meditation, and in fact, prayer is a sort of meditation in and of itself. It is common knowledge that meditation brings one closer to the divine force. It draws you closer to God and helps you connect with the Higher Energy that is all around you.

Compassion is developed via the practise of meditation, which helps one feel a deeper sense of connection to and empathy for others. As a consequence of this, you will develop more empathy and comprehension for the people around you. This, in turn, will assist you in developing stronger and more meaningful connections with the individuals in your immediate environment.

It is highly advised that you get started meditating right away if you have been feeling overwhelmed, exhausted, ill, and as like your life is going nowhere fast. Your physical well-being, your emotional state, and your state of mind will all improve as a result of your meditation practise, and as a result, your life will become richer, happier, and more satisfying.

The 7 Chakras

There are seven primary chakras, also known as energy centres, located throughout the human body. They have a significant impact on your health on several levels, including the physical, the mental, the emotional, and the spiritual. To have a life that is full of happiness, health, and pleasure, one of the most important prerequisites is to have open chakras that are in a state of balance. In the next , we will explain the history of the chakras as well as introduce the seven primary chakras. However, although the idea that energy may interact with the body is common to many cultures, the notion of the chakras is exclusive to India and was created there. When one is familiar with the seven chakras, one is also familiar with the symptoms of blockages, which interfere with the flow of energy throughout the body, as well as the techniques by which one may repair and unblock the chakras. Throughout the whole of this book, we will be talking about the primary strategies.

What Do Each of the Seven Chakras Represent?

There are seven primary chakras, which may be thought of as energy centres. They may be found everywhere from the bottom of the spine to the very top of the skull, often known as the crown. Your life may be impacted in a variety of ways depending on the chakra you focus on. It is possible for difficulties to arise in the physical, mental, emotional, and spiritual worlds if one or more of the chakras are blocked or out of balance. As you learn more about the seven primary chakras, you will become more aware of the root causes of the challenges you face in your life. The chakras of many individuals are either blocked or out of harmony. However, the tools you need to open and repair the chakras are already inside you, and you may even perform it on your own in the quiet of your own home if you like. The kind and type of blockages are important factors to consider.

When one of the body's seven chakras becomes blocked, the result is a disruption in the body's natural flow of energy. It is essential to have all of the chakras completely open and in harmony in order for energy to go through the body in the manner that it was designed to move. When a chakra is out of alignment, you will have an overabundance of one facet of your being expressed, which will have the effect of preventing other aspects from being completely expressed. We all know someone who has struggled with an addiction, whether it is to gambling, sexual activity, or both. We also know individuals who are so rational that they are unable to acknowledge the spiritual or mystical aspect of reality. These are instances of persons whose chakras are out of balance, and as a result, they display an excessive amount of one facet of their character at the detriment of other aspects of their personality.

while one studies eastern philosophy, which is really grounded in common sense, one comes to the realisation that human beings (indeed, all beings to some degree) are equally embedded among a variety of realities or facets of existence. This is one of the epiphanies that one has while studying eastern philosophy. For instance, the experience of pleasure is natural and integral to the human condition. But take a look at the people around you and ask yourself how many of them (or maybe even you) are suffering from an imbalance in this area due to their obsession with pursuing pleasure. How many individuals have you met who have allowed the pursuit of sexual pleasure, drinking, or gambling to take control of their life and, in some circumstances, cause their lives to be ruined? As we go through this book, we will see that these situations are instances of imbalances that place an emphasis on the sacral chakra at the detriment of others.

It should come as no surprise that a higher level of one's self is comprised of spiritual awareness and purpose. This is correct, without a doubt. And it is not hard to understand how a blocking of your higher self, in the form of empathy, spiritual purpose, and other such things, might lead to a fixation with the lower functions of the body, which are directed towards physical pursuits.

But let's not get ahead of ourselves; as we go on, we will get a more in-depth understanding of these topics. For the time being, let's begin familiarising ourselves with the seven primary chakras. It is possible to cure both the body and the spirit by working with the main chakras, thus it is not necessary to have knowledge of the smaller chakras. For most individuals, working with the major chakras is sufficient. Those who are interested in pursuing a more in-depth study are, of course, free to continue their education and research into the subordinate chakras. However, we shall be concentrating on the seven primary chakras throughout this book.

The seven primary chakras are detailed below, along with their Sanskrit names, the colours they represent, and their anatomical locations throughout the body. When it comes to meditation, it is essential to be aware of the colour as well as the actual position of the body, as we shall see. When doing yoga, this is also a crucial consideration. The Sanskrit names are offered for your convenience as a reference so that if you happen to come across a work that makes use of the Sanskrit terms, you will have no trouble understanding what is being discussed. Since the notion of the chakras and the study of them originated in ancient India, we also include their names for the purpose of providing a historical reference.

The seven major chakras are:

Root Chakra (Muladhara): Located at the base of the spine. The associated color is red.

Sacral Chakra (Svadhishthana): Located on the front of the body just below the navel. The color is orange.

Solar Plexus (Manipura): Located in the stomach area, below the rib cage but above the navel. The color is yellow.

Heart Chakra (Anahata): Located in the center of the chest. The color is green.

Throat Chakra (Vishuddha): Located at the base of the throat. The color is blue or turquoise.

Third Eye (Ajna): Located just above the eyes in the center of the brow. The color is indigo.

Crown Chakra (Sahasrara): Located on the crown of the head. The colors are purple, white, and gold.

Notice the progression of the colors, from red to blue to purple; this is no accident! The colors move through the colors of the rainbow. Scientists tell us that these colors correspond to the energy of light. Green light is more energetic than yellow or red light, for example. In the study of the chakras, higher energy vibrations correspond to more spiritual aspects of being. As we get into the details of each of the chakras, you will come to understand the energy associations and why each has higher energy and color than the previous chakra.

The locations in the body are not accidental, either. The closer you are to the earth, the more the physical aspects of being are emphasized. This is not to say that one is more important than the other in any fundamental sense. A truly spiritually awakened person has all aspects of their being awakened and in balance.

Although we describe the seven chakras as having physical locations, the energies associated with them are spiritual in nature. Therefore, it has a subtler quality, even though it is as real as anything in the universe if not more real.

Put Obstacles In Front Of Yourself

Create your own personal objectives to ensure that you continue to challenge yourself beyond your current capabilities. Challenge your conventional ways of thinking and make the most of your existing skills. This does not necessarily have to cover things of a sensitive nature. A few examples of this would include learning a new language, beginning a new pastime, or even gaining the ability to play an instrument musically.

This will help you continue to extend your horizons, bring you into touch with a variety of individuals, and build both your body and your intellect. You will be putting your intuitive abilities to use, which in turn will be beneficial to those abilities since you will be expanding your knowledge. As you continue to learn new things and improve your talents, you will also find that you become more modest. When you are in a condition of humility, you naturally develop greater empathy and gratitude for others.

When you find yourself in a challenging situation, take advantage of the opportunity to learn more about who you are and how you engage with the world around you. You will end up being thankful for the experiences you've had because they will cause you to mature in ways that you never would have without the obstacle being in your path.

Get out of what you consider to be your safe zone.

When you are thrust into unfamiliar circumstances, it forces you to depend more on your own intuitive abilities to guide you through the maze of uncharted territory. Travel is an exceptionally wonderful approach to accomplish this goal. Not only will you gain knowledge about new locations, but you will also get the opportunity to interact with people who come from cultures other than your own. Your perspective and scope of thinking will be expanded as a result of this.

You will also be better able to comprehend a wider variety of people, which will come in useful since it will make it easier for you to assist various categories of individuals. A sense of gratitude for the individual differences that individuals possess will develop. Your ability to listen will also improve as you gain more knowledge about the different locations and individuals you encounter. Your ability to develop creative solutions to problems is stimulated when you are required to look at issues from a perspective that is unfamiliar to you. It's possible that doing so will help you improve your problem-solving abilities while also educating you on new topics.

This will compel you to overcome any anxiety that you have towards the unknown. This dread is crippling and has no basis in reality. The fact that you do not know what to anticipate is the root cause of your anxiety towards the performance of particular tasks. On the other hand, going through challenging new experiences will almost always leave you stronger, and you'll find that the associated fear is no longer relevant to your life. Your psychic abilities will flourish to the extent that you are able to reduce the amount of fear in your life.

The Meditations That Only Take Five Minutes

In this , we are going to talk about the many different kinds of five-minute meditations that you may do if you have five minutes to spare. Please be aware that several of these meditations for five minutes may be utilised interchangeably, and that one need not be all that severe in sticking to keeping them to the categories that have been set above for them. Please take this into consideration.

The proverb states that "the early bird gets the worm." It is true that the morning is often the most beneficial time to meditate, simply because this is the time of day when one's mind is the clearest and most alert. Let us take a look at some five-minute meditations that we can use to effectively start the day and gear ourselves up for a more improved state of mind, one that will help us to demonstrate high levels of productivity at the workplace. Let us also look at some meditations that we can use to successfully start the day and gear ourselves up for a more enhanced state of mind.

A little meditation that may be done first thing in the morning, lasting only five minutes.

The first thing you need to do is make sure that your mind is clear and not in the least way foggy when you sit down to meditate in the morning. To ensure that you are "completely" awake before you eat breakfast, you should wash your face with water that has been warmed to body temperature. After that, do a few gentle stretches, and you will be ready to begin your meditation practise.

Step Two: As was said before, in order to get the most beneficial outcomes possible, you should go into the area that you have "designated" as your meditation room and sit there for a while. Make sure you are in the most comfortable posture you can sit in for a period of five minutes, whether you want to sit on a chair, a cushion on the floor, or even both; the time limit for this exercise is five minutes.

Step Three: Take in and exhale a full, natural breath with each inhale and exhale. You could find it helpful to have a private conversation with yourself in which you say something along the lines of "Breathing in, I am aware of the breath entering my body." As I let out my breath, I am conscious of my breath leaving my body.

The fourth step is to put your palm on your stomach and observe the natural rise and fall of your tummy as you breathe in and out.

Step Five: By the third or fourth breath, you should become aware of the slowing down and deepening of your breath. This should happen by the time you reach this step. Simply placing your hand over your stomach will provide you with a feeling of protection and serenity. At this point, you may want to have a private conversation with yourself in which you say something along the lines of "Taking a deep breath,

I smile at the prospect of the new day ahead." Exhaling, I have complete confidence that today is going to be an amazing day.

Before you leave for the workplace in the morning, you will have no trouble doing this task at all. In addition to that, it will establish the tone for the rest of the day and kickstart your productivity to a level that is unrivalled during the course of the day!

You do not have to restrict that kind of meditation to just taking place in the early morning. In point of fact, you may even partake in the activity in its traditional setting in the workplace, whenever you discover that you may have a few minutes free between your various tasks. Let's have a look at something appropriate for the workplace!

5. EXITING THE STATE OF MEDITATION

If you come out of meditation in the right manner, the new sensations you experienced while it will linger for a considerable amount of time and even seep into the rest of your life.

There are three processes involved in exiting meditation in a proficient manner.

- Give some thought to how successful your meditation was.

Consider everything that you've been able to accomplish in such a short amount of time throughout this session.

Since one of the goals of meditation is to increase one's self-awareness, you should take some time to reflect on both the aspects of one's life that went well and those that were challenging. Keep that sense of composure you have and prepare your future moves so that they are consistent with it. You will discover that you are able to cope with your issues in a more productive manner. Additionally, establish a mental note of the ways in which you would want to alter the next time you sit down to meditate.

- Reiterate your efforts to spread feelings of friendliness.

Do you remember what I said about having an ethereal attitude? It's all about having positive thoughts about other people and desiring the best for everyone you know and care about. You completed this task at the conclusion of your session, and it is recommended that you do so on subsequent occasions. This will assist you in maintaining that feeling of lightness in your body.

• As you open your eyes and move out of the meditative position, make an effort to maintain your sensitivity to the energy that is being carried through the body by the breath.

It is not true that the practise of meditation is no longer important just because it has ended. Instead of allowing yourself to get disconnected the instant it is over, cling to the sensation you had. Focus your attention during the last few seconds of your meditation on the sensations that are occurring inside you. As you start to open your eyes, make an effort to extend the scope of your comprehension.

Because it has so many beneficial consequences on our lives, meditation is a very beneficial practise. This occurs due to the fact that it does not terminate when your session terminates. If you conclude it in the right way, you will have more energy for the rest of the day. Keep in mind that everything will work out in the end.

The Mental Process And Ideas

Imagine a railway or tube station where passengers stand in queue at the entrance while awaiting the arrival of their respective train. After boarding the train, they wait for it to arrive at their station and are then transported to their final location. There are some who go to the west, while others head east, north, or south. They are transported away from the station in whichever direction they go, regardless of where they turn. An employee of the station is now observing everything that is taking place while they are seated at their assigned workstation. There is a significant amount of activity taking on at this time. This individual is unmoved by the flurry of activity that is occurring around them and is not easily distracted by the constant stream of people entering and exiting the area.

This whole thing is meant to be seen as a metaphor for the mind. The train carriages that whisk us away from the here and now are our thoughts. A number of our ideas take us back in time and lead us in that path. Fear underlies the thinking that contributes to this behaviour. The future is brought to our attention by other ideas. The expectation that something will happen drives the ideas that are the cause of this. A person who meditates and has the ability to concentrate and still the mind is comparable to the employee at the station. The person who practises meditation, much like the worker at the station, is not transported to either the past or the future. Instead, they keep their consciousness rooted in the here and now. It's not that they are unaware of thinking; on the contrary, they are acutely conscious of it. What they don't do, though, is interact with the notion;

rather, they continue to act as a witness to it. This metaphor is not without its flaws due to the fact that time itself is an illusion that is produced by the mind. Both the past and the future are illusions. The only thing that exists is the consciousness of what is going on.

Another illusion that the mind creates for us is that of thinking, in addition to giving us the idea that time really exists. The vast majority of us are susceptible to allowing our ideas to control not just how we feel but also the decisions we end up making. Our ideas give us the impression that they have power over us. The reason for this is because we tend to give our ideas a personality or connect ourselves with them. Breaking through this illusion and coming to the understanding that our ideas are not who we are is one of the most significant effects of meditation. In point of fact, our ideas have no influence. Because we are the ones who give our ideas their power—which we do by paying attention to them—they are dependent on us.

In addition, our ideas do not have any significance of their own; they are neither positive nor negative. Instead, it is up to us to lend significance to our own ideas. Our ideas are nothing more than snippets of information, much to how a computer receives information from a programme that it is running. It is our own ability to ascribe meaning to an idea that determines whether that thinking is "good" or "bad."

In the practise of meditation, it is a frequent misconception that your mind needs to be empty of ideas; however, this is not the case. Thoughts in and of themselves are not problematic; what you should try to avoid doing is devoting attention to your thoughts. When you are meditating, you should avoid resisting anything at all. Allow whatever it is that you are experiencing to bring itself to your conscious attention. Do not attempt to modify anything or have any expectations about what should occur. You are the consciousness of everything of experience, including thoughts, perceptions, and sensations. This includes everything that is happening right now. Allow everything that is happening to you to play out before you.

You are the observer of all experience, yet you are not changed in any way by any of it. There is not a single idea or feeling that can hurt you. Your awareness shines a light on every aspect of your existence. You, as consciousness, are comparable to a ray of sunshine that illuminates the snow-covered landscape. The light shines through the glistening snow, yet it is undisturbed by the subzero temperatures.

Beliefs are a sort of cognition in which we have formed a degree of conviction about, and this level of certainty may be called "absolute." Our worldview shapes not just what we pay attention to in the world but also what we choose to ignore, the choices we make, and the way we experience life. The lens through which we see the world is coloured by the convictions we have, much like a pair of sunglasses. As is the case with ideas, beliefs do not possess any force of their own; rather, they get all of their influence from the attention that we give them. In addition, the ideas and opinions that we have are not correct nor incorrect; they just transmit information about the experiences that we have had. It is up to each of us to give our ideas and convictions some kind of significance.

Within the Buddhist tradition, the mind is often referred to as the "monkey mind." Our thoughts are always racing, much like a monkey's. Your mind will go from being a monkey's mind to a quiet mind once you are able to attain the stage in meditation when you are able to be the witness of every experience without being caught up in it. Your most insightful realisations are going to come to you while you are in this frame of mind. Because of this, we may say that the goal of practising Buddhist meditation is to train the mind in such a way that we become in command of it, rather than having our minds be in charge of us. This is because our minds should serve us, not the other way around.

Positive Meditation May Help Improve Both Your Spiritual And Emotional Outlook On Life. Here Are Some Of The Secrets To Doing So.

When you have a more optimistic perspective on life, you will experience increased levels of happiness and contentment. When you have a more optimistic perspective on life, you become a beam of sunshine to the people who know you, and both your life and the connections you have become usually easier, happier, and more rewarding. How to Become More cheerful, Compassionate, Emotionally Supportive, and Spiritual Here are some recommendations on how to become more cheerful, compassionate, emotionally supportive, and spiritual:

1. Always treat other people the way you would like to be treated yourself. This is known as the "Golden Rule." Keep in mind that God dwells deep inside each of us. Whatever you do to other people, remember that you are also doing it to your Creator since our bodies are the temples in which the Divine resides. Be kind and patient with others. Always keep in mind that the majority of us are waging a struggle, and because of this, be thoughtful to others.

2. Focus on the here and now; there's no use in wasting time lamenting things that have already happened. Let go of your errors and the things you regret from the past. It is essential to ignore one's worries and just take pleasure in the here and now.

3. Gratitude is a really powerful practise that can bring so much pleasure into your life, so make sure you cultivate an attitude of gratitude. When you count your blessings instead of your problems, you become closer to God and find it much simpler to take a more optimistic attitude on life.

4. Quit making unfair comparisons between yourself and other people; we all face unique challenges. Stop making comparisons between your life and the lives of other people; everyone of us has a unique burden to bear. Comparison on a continual basis will only serve to bring about sadness and discontent.

5. Visualise What You desire - When you visualise what you desire, you are putting your attention on that rather

than on what you do not want. You'll be able to unwind and enjoy yourself more as a result of this. Additionally, this exercise has been shown to have the capacity to bring you whatever it is in life that you want.

6. Make a habit of laughing. Watch comedies on Netflix or YouTube, tell jokes often, and think back on amusing times in your life. If you laugh more, you'll find that it makes you happier and more optimistic.

Maintaining a state of mental tranquilly and being optimistic need to be second nature to you. You will unquestionably have a better life if you make meditation a regular practise and participate in other activities that teach you to appreciate the here and now.

Meditation With A Guided For The Purification Of The Mind

This exercise is performed with the intention of ridding the body and mind of the harmful vibrations and ideas that we have built up over the course of the days. You'll get the finest results if you do it every day.

Pick a location that is uncomplicated and devoid of any potential distractions. Put yourself in a relaxed state by getting into a comfortable posture. You have twenty seconds to close your eyes and focus on your breathing. Take a long, deep breath in and hold it for ten seconds before releasing it.

Relax your body and realign your spine after holding this position for twenty seconds. Put your hands and feet up to relax. Imagine that there is a bright point of light beaming just over your head and sending out waves of comfort and joy.

Feel the tension in your face melt away as a smile spreads over your face and a sense of joy fills your expression.

Take a moment to breathe deeply (around 20 seconds). Imagine that this bright and gentle heat is spreading throughout your whole body and completely purifying all of the dense, bad energy that you have generated and received from places and people throughout the course of your lifetime. Inhale, then exhale for twenty seconds.

Now, that little point of light mutates into a tide of healing energy that washes over your whole body and extends outward. Take a deep breath and hold it for twenty seconds.

Now, as you concentrate on this, you should feel your thoughts of melancholy, anxiety, dread, and concern gradually dissipate and be replaced with ideas of deep serenity, harmony, and protection. Have confidence. Observe how your strength and vitality totally replenish itself with each breath you take. A deep breath (for twenty seconds) Feel yourself being safeguarded by the light that is encompassing your body and thoroughly cleansing your thoughts.

Recognise the buoyancy and calmness that is currently present in both your body and your thinking. Take another deep breath in (twenty-twenty seconds). Give yourself permission to sense the rejuvenation taking place in both your body and your mind. Every single cell and organ is experiencing a full revitalization right now.

Feel your shoulders loosening up and your body stretching out completely. Take slow, deep breaths in and out over the next thirty seconds.

As your mind becomes more at ease and your body relaxes, you should experience a tremendous sense of lightness throughout your whole body. All of the discomforts go away.

Hold your breath for twenty seconds. Observe how your vibration gradually increases on its own. Experience a sense of serenity and tranquillity. Keep up your even and deep breathing for the next thirty seconds.

Begin by moving gently while stretching and stretching every muscle in your body. Take another full breath and wait thirty seconds. Learn to be aware of both yourself and the world around you.

What exactly does it mean to be a Sufi?

What exactly does this term signify in all seriousness? S U F I..., the expression makes me think of a cryptic spell word or a cryptic chant. When it comes to the derivation of the phrase, there are several meanings, some of which are ambiguous: It derives its meanings of "wool" and "purity" and "transparency" from the Arabic word sûf. Early mystics such as John the Baptist and Jesus of Nazareth, both of whom may peace be with them, wore clothes made of wool, and they are considered to have been members of the Sufi order. The meaning of the name "Sufiya" is "one chosen as intimate friend (of God)". In addition to this, it is stated that they are the heirs of the disciples who used to dwell in the courtyard of the prophet Muhammad. The majority of people, as far as the word "Sufi" is known, associate a vision of whirling oriental dervishes dressed in white with high hats whenever they hear the phrase "Sufi." However, if we simply allude to this, it continues to be a cliché. After all, the formation of Sufi communities dates back to the beginning of the first century after Christ. Since that time, substantially more than one hundred Sufi orders, also known as turuq, have emerged, practically all of which are still active in the modern day. The outward aspect of the members may vary, but the interior aim and attitude of all Sufis is the same: to seek and practise Divine Wisdom and Love. This is also the most concise explanation of what "Sufism" means that is conceivable. It is possible to trace its origins back to the beginning of human history and find evidence of it in every tradition.

An ancient metaphor goes something like this:

Adam is credited as planting the seed of Sufism, which then flourished during the time of Noah, matured under Abraham's leadership, started to mature during Moses' leadership, achieved its full development during Jesus' leadership, and finally produced the pure wine via Muhammad's leadership.

HazratInayat-Khan, a musician and mystic who lived from 1882 to 1927, is considered to be one of the most important figures in the Sufi religion. He is the first person to symbolise a global kind of Sufism, which is transcendent of both faiths and boundaries. We owe it to this great master, musician, and mystic who lived at the beginning of the 20th century for the message of Sufism to have obtained a vast distribution in a global spirituality at that time. His "Sufi Message" is a collection of lectures, poetry, and aphorisms that spans 14 volumes and is directed at the Western world. This scholarly text covers all aspects of a spiritual life as well as the mystical teachings that come from the Sufi tradition. It is filled with invaluable insights that have a captivating beauty and a caring heart. The spiritual "acupoints" that are being built as a consequence of the work done by Inayat Khan, the Sufi Order, the Sufi Movement, and the Sufi Way, and more especially the Inayati Order, are accessible to anybody who has an interest in participating. By focusing their attention on the Sufi path and acting in accordance with an initiation received from a teacher or Shaikh, many seekers have discovered their own path and purpose in life, as well as love, harmony, and beauty, as well as healing, health, and tranquilly.

The message of Sufism is more vital now than it has ever been before because of the severe issues that mankind faces on a worldwide scale. Because they are always experiencing change, the orders and movements have been able to keep their openness and authenticity right up to the present day. If this were not the case, then dogmatism and complacency would be the norm.

Sufis are not just the mystics of Islam, but in a general sense they are also the mystical representatives of all faiths and spiritual traditions. Sufism is a branch of Islam that focuses on mystical practises. They have always been the ones to shake people out of their complacency and serve as admonishers of the times in which they lived. They are the ones that adore and sing the praises of the truth and hold the service of others near and dear to their hearts.

Meditations With A Guided Focus On Happiness

I. Meditation on the State of Mind at Bliss

Turn down the lights, and choose a secluded spot where you may relax in peace.

Create a comfortable environment for yourself while also relaxing your muscles and putting yourself in a calm condition.

Place your hands on your lap, and shut your eyes as gently as you can.

First, take a few deep breaths, and then just relax.

Allow yourself to make a connection with your inner being while keeping your eyes closed. Get completely absorbed in your own ideas and emotions. You will eventually become more conscious of your surroundings as the world around you begins to recede into the background.

Take advantage of this state of relaxation and prepare both your mind and heart for what is ahead. Allow yourself a few minutes to relax and get your thoughts organised.

Put all of your worries to one side for the time being since you are now free from all of your obligations. You won't be affected by your issues here; this place is a refuge of peace.

During meditation, if you find that your thoughts have wandered, you should simply return your attention back to your breathing. Take some deep breaths, settle down, and find solace in the calm that is inside you.

Remind yourself that you are the one in charge of the situation. You may return to your own world at any time by doing nothing more than opening your eyes.

Inhale and exhale slowly and deeply. Take a deep breath in and then out. Take a deep breath in and then out. Take a deep breath in and then out.

You have a greater sense of calm presently. You are completely unconcerned about anything in the world.

Once again, be sure to take calm, deep breaths. Take a deep breath in and then out. Take a deep breath in and then out. Take a deep breath in and then out.

Right now, you have a sense of serenity and tranquilly. Imagine the best possible outcomes.

Once again, be sure to take calm, deep breaths. Take a deep breath in and then out. Take a deep breath in and then out. Take a deep breath in and then out.

It seems as if you are drawing ever-nearer to the state of ecstasy with each breath that you take.

When you imagine happy thoughts, you may physically feel your heart growing larger in your chest.

You are now prepared to go on this guided trip to your own personal paradise, a haven of peace that you may refer to as your very own.

Permit yourself to conjure up joyful ideas in your thoughts. Don't try to push things. As you take long, steady breaths, give yourself permission to let things happen naturally.

Free yourself from your inhibitions and set aside your expectations. Give your imagination permission to conjure up whatever pictures it pleases.

If the visuals aren't coming to you readily, you might try visualising your perfect environment via your senses instead. How does the air make you feel when it touches your skin? What type of aroma do you pick up on here? Do you hear anything at all? Permit yourself to get completely immersed in the event.

Imagine that you are perched atop a hill, and that in front of you is an open green field.

Imagine that the sun is warming your face and the rest of your body.

Imagine the tickling sensation of the grass on the tender flesh of your bare feet.

Imagine that you are far away and you hear bird sounds. Try to picture the soothing sound of a nearby babbling stream.

Imagine being at ease in this setting for a moment. Imagine you had an infinite amount of time to take in the beauty of your surroundings without any interruptions.

Imagine for a moment that you are protected in this building that you call home.

Imagine being completely happy and fulfilled, with no desire or need for anything else in the world.

Please allow yourself some time to sit back and take in the breathtaking views and tranquil atmosphere. Walk around and get a feel for each of the steps.

You will experience an even deeper sense of relaxation and tranquilly as you make your way through this mental paradise.

Picture a large tree with wide leaves growing close to where you are right now. Take baby steps in the direction of the tree until you arrive at your destination below it.

Take note that the tree is laden with delicious fruits in a variety of sizes and forms that are dangling from it. This unique tree produces fruit that, when consumed, will bestow upon you a variety of distinct supernatural abilities.

Extend your hand and pluck a fruit from the branch that is resting on the ground. Examine the piece of fruit that you now have in your grasp for a bit. Feel the touch of it and the weight of it in your palm in addition to just looking at the colour of it.

Take a bite out of the fruit and allow it to satiate both your physical and mental hunger.

As you continue to chew and swallow the fruit, you will become aware of an increasing warmth throughout your body. The feeling will start in your upper chest and go to your heart, followed by spreading to your arms and legs.

Foster this sensation of love and joy that you're experiencing in your body. Put an end to your thoughts and concentrate on the sensation instead. You will experience a light that is otherworldly and a feeling of happiness that will spread through your whole body.

Take another taste of your fruit, but this time focus on savouring each and every mouthful you take. Allow the feeling to get stronger as the flavour develops.

When you take a third mouthful, you will notice that it radically alters the way you see the world. You are experiencing a level of joy that is unmatched by anything else in the world right now. Permit the warmth that is contained inside you to emerge and permeate the world around you.

Take in the serene atmosphere and savour this time set aside for reflection on your own happiness.

You may decide how long you wish to spend meditating.

Simply opening your eyes is all that is required to bring your meditation to a close when you are ready. Before going back to your regular schedule, you should give yourself a few minutes to relax and get used to being awake before getting back to work.

The Composition Of The Elements Within The Human Hand And Mudras

In certain ancient societies, it was thought that separate energy centres for the five elements that make up the world—air, space, earth, fire, and water—could be found in different parts of the human body, namely in the hands. When you link your fingers and hands in distinct hand gestures, also known as mudras, you influence the five components and the different sections of your brain to bring about diverse outcomes. This is because the different nerves in your fingers connect to different parts of your brain.

Your thumb symbolises space, your index finger represents air, your middle finger represents fire, your ring finger represents water, and your pinky finger represents earth.

You may make the most of your practise and get the most out of it by just placing your hands on your lap, but you can also do other mudras to make the most of your practise and get the most out of it. The following are some of the most effective mudras that you may practise to develop your spirituality, knowledge, and awareness, as well as to improve your physical health.

The Gyan Mudra.

Because it unites the components of space and air, this mudra will expand your understanding, as well as your intuitive powers and awareness. Touch the tip of your index finger with the pad of your thumb while maintaining the straight positions of your other fingers. While you are meditating, give it a try for ten to sixty seconds at a time, or even longer if you can.

The posture of Buddhi Mudra.

This mudra helps cleanse your mind and provides you with insight into your ambitions, objectives, and aspirations. In addition, by constantly practising it, you may develop your speaking ability and talk with total confidence to express your opinions as it unites the components of space and earth. This is because it is a bridge between the two. To perfect this skill, touch your thumb and pinky finger together while maintaining the straight positions of your other three fingers.

The Mudra of Dhyana

This position incorporates all five aspects and is an effective tool for improving your ability to focus on activities at hand, calming agitated nerves, and gaining access to a place of inner serenity. In addition to this, it is beneficial to your health. In order to perfect it, you should position your right hand so that it is resting on top of the palm of your left hand, and then delicately link your two thumbs together.

You may improve the overall efficacy of the practise by adopting any one of these three stances and doing it. Now that we've covered the first two elements of the posture, let's move on to the last three points in the next .

Insolvent, Bitter, And Shattered To The Core

Moab was the beginning of a sad new in Naomi's life. Her family had gone there in the hopes of finding safety and deliverance from the hunger. The choice ultimately led to Naomi's death, along with the deaths of her husband and two boys. She was left destitute, with her heart shattered, and resentful. Because of this, she instructs the ladies of Bethlehem to stop calling her Naomi, which means "pleasant," and instead to refer to her as "Mara," which means "bitter." She asserts that she left full, but the LORD caused her to return empty. In her mind, the LORD had transformed into her enemy, and he was now testifying against her before the heavenly tribunals.

Naomi's theology of suffering is correct in that it correctly identifies the providential hand of God behind her misfortune. Her calamities were not the result of random occurrences. The all-powerful LORD decided to do this beforehand. She is suffering at the hands of a God who is both benevolent and compassionate. This reality, rather than being a source of solace, is a source of bitterness. As Naomi considers the bleak conditions of her existence, she loses sight of her sacred identity as a person who is loved by God and is part of the covenant. She disregards the fact that Romans 8:28 states that all things work together for the benefit of those who love God and are called according to the purpose that God has for them. Because of Naomi's distorted perspective on her tribulations, she gives herself a new identity and calls herself Mara. However, no one ever refers to her by that name at any point during the whole of the book of Ruth. God is not an adversary of hers. Even in the most trying times, God is on the side of those he has chosen to be his people through Jesus Christ. Even when Naomi forgets who she is as a holy person and believes that she is a failure, the people of God are aware of the truth. They are aware that this gloomy elderly person is only a child of God who is having a terrible day.

All of the biblical characters, including Joseph in the pit, Job with sores on the street, Jonah in the stomach of the fish, and Daniel in the lion's cave, went through difficult times. Despite this, they were aware that God was working through this situation to accomplish something positive. In his book A Divine Cordial, the Puritan Thomas Watson penned the following passage: "To know that nothing hurts the godly, is a matter of comfort; but to be assured that all things which fall out shall cooperate for their good, that their crosses shall be turned into blessings, that showers of affliction water the withering root of their grace and make it flourish more— this may fill their hearts with joy until they run over!" After all, the same hand of God that caused Naomi to suffer was the same hand that led her to Bethlehem without incident.

What Is The Shakti Of The Kundalini?

The Kundalini force is a mysterious energy that resides deep inside each of us and has the capacity to broaden our awareness. Thereare three primary aspects that constitute the Kundalini power. One consists of one's breath, sexuality, and mental state.

Because of this, the science of pranayama places a significant emphasis on breathing techniques. The expansion of pranic energy inside us is accomplished via the use of breath as the carrier. When there is a shift in the regular rhythm of respiration, there is also a shift in the mental state that is occurring inside us. Sexuality is an additional factor that contributes to the kundalinishakti. Because of this, brahmcharya, sometimes known as celibacy, is accorded a great deal of significance. The spiritual practise of sadhana should always include the maintenance of one's sexual power. However, this does imply that one need to become obsessive with the subject in question. When it comes to spiritual practises, moderation is really essential. When engaging in sexual activities, we need to refrain from overindulging. The mind is the third significant component of the kundalini energy. Our state of mind is constantly unsettled. The first critical step, therefore, is learning how to quiet the mind so that the spiritual energies may grow in a positive direction.

A yogi is someone who has mastered the art of raising their awareness by directing the energy of their kundalini serpent to travel in a progressive direction. The practise of Kriya yoga meditation is essential for expanding our level of awareness. In the Bhagavad Gita,

Lord Krishna teaches Arjuna the Kriya Yoga Meditation Technique that we will be discussing here. In the Bhagavad Gita, there is a shloka that explains to us how the pranic energies that are contained inside us are taken by the inhalation and exhalation of breath.

The most important issue at this point is how to recognise the spiritual elements that are already present inside us.

There is only one approach that can absolutely guarantee accurate results when analysing the spiritual energy that are present inside us. This practise is known as mindfulness.

What exactly does "mindfulness" mean?

Practising mindfulness is paying attention to our own mental state in the here and now. How our ideas go around inside of us. When we focus our attention on our inner minds and really look, we can always see thoughts flowing around inside of us. Thoughts come and go as they please. Memories from the past and hopes for the future are always moving around inside of us. The thoughts that we have are like beads strung together. Therefore, there is an empty space between the two beads on the string. During meditation, we are instructed to focus our attention on the space between two beads.

Because of this, when we meditate, we must make an effort to stay in the here and now. Our minds are always trying to force us to live in the past or the future.

The passage of time may also be depicted internally by the movement of our thoughts.

How do you define time?

Time is the agent of transformation. The slower the flow of ideas inside us, the slower we are able to conceptualise the passage of time. If we can bridge the little chasm that exists between two ideas, then we will be able to eradicate the passage of time.

Alternative Methods Of Meditation

There are many different ways to practise meditation. It is possible for it to be active, particularly when the mind and the body are together. It also might consist of doing nothing more than sitting there and not thinking at all. Both yoga and Tai chi, which originate in India and China respectively, are examples of different civilizations' applications of the notion of movement meditation. Visualisation and deep breathing are two practises that may help bring the mind and the body together. As a consequence of this, the dynamic body-mind systems are beneficial to an individual's overall health.

You are able to meditate when you practise yoga because it brings the mind, body, breath, and spirit into balance. In addition, maintaining focus is essential for every stance.

In Tai chi, the coordination of the mind and body is achieved via the use of movements that are both balanced and relaxing. This practise leads to improvements in both one's health and one's knowledge of oneself.

The mind-body systems provide a person with a multitude of useful advantages. They not only enhance mental alertness and attention but also offer flexibility and suppleness to the body as well.

Not Giving Any Thought to It

You are already familiar with the four (4) crucial stages that are involved in meditation. You may be wondering whether it is even possible to meditate if all you do is sit quietly and try not to think about anything. Yes, very much so!

"Just sitting" is what zazen literally implies. This is one of the most important practises in Zen Buddhism, and it is traditionally carried out with one's back to a wall in order to block off any potential distractions. At this point, you will not be required to visualise any particular topic, visuals, or symbols. The purpose of doing zazen is to simply watch what is going on in your mind without allowing your attention to be drawn away by your own ideas.

It is encouraged that during zazen, you think about absolutely nothing at all. You may also bring your complete consciousness to the act of watching your breath. The goal of this kind of meditation is to assist you attain mental calm by training you to exert control over your thoughts. Imagine a monkey that is always talking. Are you aware of how frustrating it may be when they hop from one branch to another? They never stop moving and never stop moving once they start. Buddhism likens this to a mind that has not been trained. A mind that is crowded just skips from one concept to the next, much like a monkey that is always chattering. Because of this, you find that you have a lot of thoughts, which in turn causes you tension and anxiety.

The good news is that you may learn to silence the chattering monkey inside you by training yourself to be aware of the stream of ideas that are running through your mind. And this is something that may be accomplished by meditating.

Is it true that being sedentary is a waste of time? It is a fallacy to believe that sitting still and doing nothing at all is only a waste of valuable time. If you are used to leading a hectic lifestyle, sitting still and doing nothing at all may seem uncomfortable at first. You may train your mind to be more productive by sitting motionless for long periods of time. After an emotionally taxing experience, such as an exam at school or a presentation at work, it is similar to giving your mind a chance to recharge. Recharging one's mind and body with even just a few minutes of alone each day is beneficial. This is not at all a productive use of one's time. Instead, you are efficiently using the time that you have available.

The vast majority of individuals are guilty of this, yet they are really doing themselves a tremendous favour by doing so. Therefore, make it a habit to sit motionless and give yourself some time to yourself every day. The advantages are incredible, to say the least.

Find some space in your mind.

If you often get the impression that your brain is crowded with a great number of unpleasant ideas, it is possible that the moment has come for you to create some mental space. Learn to halt whenever you become aware that there is just a little gap between the conclusion of one idea and the beginning of the next one. This lull in activity, however brief it may be, has the potential to significantly improve the quality of your life. It is similar to making an effort to mentally relax, and with practise, you will find that your mind becomes less cluttered.

Your current state of consciousness

Consider the contents of your mind, including your ideas and everything else that pops into your head, to be a stream of consciousness. To begin meditating and bringing peace to your mind, just sit quietly and observe how each idea arises and passes away. Give it a go for a few minutes and pay attention to how it affects you during that time. You could feel self-conscious when you first start the meditation session, but after a while, everything will start to seem more typical and natural to you. When you meditate in this way, you will find that in a very short period of time, long-forgotten memories will come flooding back to you, and ideas for the future will begin to take shape. You could even stumble onto forgotten memories that you were completely unaware of in the past.

Observe that when your mind is untrained, everything seems to be a jumble of confused elements; these are ideas and connections that are lingering in your mind that are not linked to one another and are unusual. If, on the other hand, you have a mind that has been taught, the flow of ideas will be organised, producing order inside your mind. When you have mastered this skill, you will no longer be in the same position as the babbling monkey that was discussed previously.

Alterations Made To The Brain

Meditation is something that has been practised by Buddhists for what seems like millennia now. Monks are brought up with the tradition of its good benefits, notably its ability to strengthen one's inner fortitude and achieve the knowledge that is necessary for extended spiritual practise. To summarise, Buddhist monks see meditation in the same way as Christians view prayer. In contrast, Buddhists seek a deep connection with their inner selves in order to bring the whole force of the mind under complete control. Christians, on the other hand, are trying to establish a relationship with the presence of the divine; this is the primary distinction between the two religions.

Neuroscientists have recently had the opportunity to peer directly into the brains of practitioners in order to gain a physical look at how meditation changes the activity of the brain. These technological developments occurred very recently. For instance, neuroscientists have been able to witness, via the use of MRI scanning equipment, that meditation helps to develop the brain by strengthening connections between different types of brain cells. According to the findings of a research that was published in 2012, experienced meditators had higher levels of gyrification, which is the "folding" of the cerebral cortex that happens as a natural consequence of physical development. Gyrification is thought to provide the brain the ability to do tasks more quickly than it normally would. The ability of the brain to make decisions, create memories, and concentrate would be improved, according to the gyrification theory put up by scientists.

The physical changes that take place in the brain as a direct consequence of meditation have been shown to offer a number of additional potential health benefits. For example, an increase in the thickness of the cortical layer may lead to a reduction in sensitivity to pain as well as an increase in resistance to harm. Furthermore, it is believed that regular meditation can increase the density of grey matter in the brain stem. This, in turn, can lead to improved cognitive, emotional, and immune responses as it has a positive impact on our cardiorespiratory control (our breathing and heart rate). Meditation has also demonstrated neuroprotective capabilities, meaning that it can decrease the age-related decline in grey matter and cognitive function.

Researchers have shown that the expression of particular brain metabolites that are connected to disorders like as anxiety and depression is different in meditators compared to healthy non-meditators who do not do the practise. The practise of focused attention can lead to decreased default mode network activity and connectivity – those annoying brain activities that cause our concentration to lapse and can lead to disorders such as ADHD and anxiety – and even strengthen the brain's resistance to a build-up of the beta amyloid plaques that are associated with Alzheimer's disease. This is galvanised further by the positive effects on general brain activity associated with meditation.

Finally, it has been shown that meditation has a considerable influence on the electrical activity of the brain, leading to an increase in theta and alpha EEG movements. This results in a highly developed capacity for wakeful and relaxed attention while engaging in day-to-day activities.

RemarquementsAnd Acknowledgements

I will be forever thankful to my parents for the gift of life, for the fact that they have always been there for me, and for the encouragement they have given me to investigate all of the opportunities that life has to offer. It is impossible for me to write this book without them occupying a place in my heart and permeating each and every one of our body's cells. I owe a debt of gratitude to my ancestors because they led me in the right way on the path to leading a joyful and fulfilled life, not just spiritually but also in all other parts of life.

I am thankful that you, Anurag, my husband and my closest friend, have always been there to back my ideas and my philosophy and have also been the finest critic. I am grateful to you for embracing me just the way that I am. You never fail to reignite the passion for writing that I have inside me. My angel sisters Anchita and her husband Vivek, as well as my sister Aleesha, for always being there for me, loving me, and giving me constructive feedback on how I may improve my improvisation.

I would want to express my gratitude to all of my customers, with whom I have conducted countless sessions of these meditations and soul movements, and who have done so voluntarily and without any trepidation in their thoughts or hearts. Thank you for having faith in the work that I perform. I am overjoyed that my work will soon be available to the public in the form of a book. It was their consistent and heartfelt response that served as the motivation to reach a significant audience in order to also help them.

Sincere thanks from the bottom of my heart to all of my instructors for providing the motivation and inspiration I needed to go outside of my comfort zone and realign the focus of my life towards service. They were known as Bert and Sophie Hellinger. Because of you two, I was introduced to the realm of epigenetics and the Knowing Field, which is full of limitless possibilities. I adore you both from the depths of my soul for doing this.

Above all else, I am thankful to the Universe for surrounding me with individuals who come from a variety of backgrounds, as a result of which I have been able to comprehend the many nuances of e-motions, which may be defined as energy in motion. I would want to express my gratitude to everyone who has entered my life, taken on the role of a mentor to me, and imparted invaluable nuggets of knowledge that I will remember for the rest of my life.

Making Use of This Book

This book is not only meant to be read; rather, it is intended to be experienced through doing the meditations and the soul movement. This book was written with the intention of assisting readers in intentionally re-establishing a connection with their own family systems. Reading alone is not sufficient to bring about this change. My advice is to just go with the flow and try to feel each movement in the most open-minded and in-depth way possible. For once, you owe it to yourself to throw away all of the fears and preconceptions you've built up. You should allow yourself the total freedom to be creative, but more importantly, you should allow yourself the freedom to live life. It's possible that some of you who read this book may experience something similar to entering a trance, with your mind growing more at ease and the constant stream of ideas coming to a complete halt. Additionally, this will be the most personal encounter you have ever had with the Systemic Energies.

It's possible that you feel as if you're just going through the motions of life day after day. However, this is just the top of the proverbial iceberg. Even though we aren't consciously aware of being inter-connected with so many elements and so many energies, the fact is that we are the outcome of various forces and powers coming together to create us. Even though we aren't consciously aware of being inter-connected with so many elements and so many energies. When we engage in practises such as meditation and movements of the soul, they have the ability to reach the most fundamental part of our being. one who is unfettered by any conditioning or restricting ideas, and whose only purpose in life is to take in the whole scope of the life experience. Be confident that all of these ancestors would want to be recognised, respected, and most importantly, loved. This will, of course, be the first time in a lot of people's lives that they consciously connect with their ancestors; nevertheless, this will be the case for a lot of people for the very first time.

Love is what should be the driving force in our life. Love is the one thing that, in the end, will make us feel as if we have accomplished what we set out to do. Love isn't limited to the people we're romantically involved with; rather, it has various facets that may be explored. You will feel its immensity as well as more deep ways of expressing it when you are engaging in these meditations and movement practises. Therefore, my advice to each and every one of you is to make it possible for yourself to experience the abundance that life has to give by being open to these transformations of the spirit. I have no doubt that this will assist you in shifting your attention in the direction of experiencing a more vibrant sense at the very core of your being. After all, having experiences is the most important thing in life. When you first begin your journey with this book, don't try to plan out any results or goals for yourself. It is important that you make room in your life for your ancestors, spirit guides, and the energies of the SYSTEM to direct your path.

Try One Of These Ten Varieties Of Meditation

1. Meditation techniques known as Progressive or Body Scan

The practise of body scan meditation entails paying attention to your body parts and the feelings that occur throughout your body in a progressive order beginning with your toes and working your way up to your head. You may bring awareness to your body and reflect on the tension, discomfort, or aches and pains you may be experiencing by mentally scanning your body from head to toe. Your goal should not be to totally get rid of the pain, but rather to learn to recognise it, get some insight from it, and ultimately become more skilled at managing it.

Research has shown that engaging in this particular kind of meditation on a daily basis, whether once or several times, may have a significant calming effect not just on the mind but also on the body. It starts a domino effect, which results in a decrease in the discomfort produced by inflammation, which in turn leads to a better night's sleep, reduced weariness, clearer thinking, and an overall improvement in your mood.

If you have trouble falling or staying asleep, this is an excellent meditation just before night. If you haven't gone to sleep by the time you've done going through this series of steps, you should try doing things in reverse order.

In the bathtub, with some Epsom salts and an aromatherapy lavender bubble bath, you may engage in a very beneficial kind of meditation. After adding some soothing spa music, such as ocean or nature sounds, you will be ready to go.

How to go about it

You may begin from your feet and work your way up your body till you reach your head, or you can do it the other way around. You may pinpoint specific areas of discomfort or tension by concentrating on the myriad of aches and pains you may be experiencing at now moment and then releasing them with a deep exhalation.

1. Put on clothes that is comfortable and does not impede your movement.

2. Whether you choose to sit, recline, or lay down in Savasana, do so in a comfortable posture. This step is especially important if you are doing the body scan just before going to bed.

3. Make sure you are utilising your diaphragm as you take a few long, slow breaths.

4. Redirect your thoughts to whatever it is that you are doing at this very minute

in order to stop your mind from wandering and to keep your attention on the here and now.

5. Direct your attention on either your head or your feet, depending on where you would want to begin.

6. Before moving on to the next point, make sure you have worked your way through all of the points in your body. If you begin at the very top of your head, you should work your way down to your forehead, then go on to your brows, eyes, cheekbones, ears, nose, and so on. If you are going to begin with your feet, you should begin with your toes, then go on to the soles of your feet and the arch of your feet, your heels, the top of your feet, your ankles, and so on.

7. Give a particular amount of focus and attention to any areas that are tight or unpleasant. Relax and take several deep breaths, and at the same time, envision

the pain departing via your breath at that exact area each time you exhale. This will help you to calm down and focus on your breathing.

8. Move on to the next location when the pain in the previous one begins to subside.

9. When you have finished as many repetitions as you need or have time for, return your focus back to the breath that you are taking in and out of your body.

10. If you had your eyes closed, open them now, and go into the present moment with awareness. Or, if you are already in bed, you may choose to keep them shut and have a restful night's sleep.

The Actual Process Of Meditating

You are now ready to meditate after following the instructions given in the prior to prepare yourself. Do not anticipate that you will become an expert in a single day. You are used to having ideas in your head at the time, which is a good sign. Elizabeth Gilbert tried meditation and described it in her book which was called "Eat, Pray, Love." What she discovered was that her mind fought meditation and that her thoughts leapfrogged over one another fighting actually getting into a meditative trance. This was because she had too much baggage from the past and found it difficult to actually drop any of it or let go of it. Be prepared for obstacles, since there definitely will be some.

To take in air

You should shut your eyes and take a deep breath in through both nostrils, just like you were instructed to do in a previous , but this time you should really pay attention to what you are doing. Feel the air entering your body as you count to eight as you take a deep inhale. Do not divert your attention to anything else. Your ability to meditate effectively relies on your ability to concentrate on your breathing. After counting to ten, maintain the hold on the breath, and as you exhale, you should feel all of the air coming from the upper diaphragm, exactly as we showed you in the part that was devoted to breathing techniques. Let's count one. Repeat what you just did, and as you let out your breath this time, count to 2. Continue doing this until you reach 10.

When you start meditating for the first time, you're going to notice that thoughts will come into your head. You may be able to take two or three breaths before your thoughts start to drift away from your breathing and towards other things. When that time comes, revert to step number one. Try not to let it make you feel irritated. Everyone goes through this at some point. People are so used to having ideas flowing through their brains that it is not common for them to think about nothing but their breathing instead. However, it is essential that this be the sole thing that occupies your thoughts at all times. Your thoughts that are centred in this manner assist you to replace the regular thought processes with something concrete, which enables you to step away from the challenges that are present in your life and focus your attention just on the act of breathing in and out.

Timing of the meditation session

After you have had some experience with the breathing exercises, proceed in the same manner. This is the purpose of meditation, but you shouldn't expect to achieve the pinnacle of comprehension after just a few sessions of practise. When you first start meditating, your session should only continue for a maximum of twenty minutes. However, as you get more adept at erasing ideas from your mind for longer stretches of time, you will be able to extend the length of time that you meditate to a maximum of around seventy-five minutes.

Following the completion of meditation

If after meditating you rapidly return to your regular pace of thought and hurry back into the world, you won't obtain any benefit from the practise. Take your time with this. Make it a habit to gradually restore your calm as you go about your daily activities, such as folding your rug, putting away your pillow, and so on. The advantages of meditation will be maximised if you do this.

The Art of Walking Meditation

Find a peaceful spot in the garden where you won't be bothered and use it as your training ground for this. If you have access to a nearby park that is quite secluded, this might be an excellent location for your event. You are going to focus, just as you did before, on the manner that you are breathing. Your head should be gazing in the direction of the ground as you walk, maintaining a straight back like you did previously.

This kind of meditation involves more distractions, but some individuals find it easier to connect to than sitting motionless and attempting to concentrate on their own. The focus should be on the breathing rather than the walking while you are doing this, and the circles you walk in may be of a size that is not too small. Because after you have had enough, you simply sit in a calm location for a few moments to find your way back into the world of thought, and you will find that your head will be clearer, and you will discover that you are able to make decisions more easily, and that your mind won't be so cluttered. This is useful for business people who have a lot of nervous energy between meetings or before a conference.

Meditation focused on being mindful

This is something that I always turn to. The practise of mindful meditation is a way of life. In other words, you do not assign any weight to ideas relating to the past or thoughts relating to the future. Your meditation would be more concentrated on an item, and you would just watch life without passing judgement on it. It's possible that you have a statue of Buddha or some other lovely object in your garden that you may focus your attention on. This particular style of meditation does not need you to shut your eyes; yet, maintaining a steady breathing pattern is of utmost significance during the practise. Put all of your attention on that one thing, and try to push every other idea out of your head. Concentrate on your breathing as you would with the other ways if you are having trouble with that activity.

Meditation is not the only way to practise mindfulness; it may also be done in other ways. Consider this: the next time you eat, pay attention to the various tastes and textures. When you are walking someplace, take the time to look about you and appreciate the world around you. This is a really excellent technique to become highly attentive, but the point of this exercise is not to become observant. It's all about gratitude and having a positive attitude, and that matters more than anything else. You end up being more patient and understanding as a result. You develop the ability to look on the bright side of life, and the meditation works to assist reinforce this optimistic outlook.

Listening to your body and replacing negative thoughts with observations about what is going on in the world around you are both key components of the practise of mindfulness. You are in the role of an observer. You replace every idea in your head with a topic, like eating, walking, or watching. Because of this, there is no place in your head for negative thoughts.

Practising Mindfulness Each And Every Day

It is likely that as you spend more time practising mindfulness, you will notice that you are becoming nicer, more peaceful, and more patient with others. Because of these transformations in your experience, it's likely that other aspects of your life may also undergo changes.

You may become more playful by practising mindfulness, which can also help you get the most out of having a long conversation with a friend over a cup of tea and then winding down for a restful night's sleep. This week, give these four exercises a try:

Meditations That Are Easy And Guided

1. An Easy Breathing Meditation for People Just Starting Out

This activity may assist in lowering levels of tension, anxiety, and other unfavourable feelings, calming you down when you feel your anger rising, and improving your ability to focus attention.

2. An Exploration of the Body in Order to Foster Mindfulness

An abbreviated form of the mindfulness meditation practise that can help you relax your body and bring your focus to your mind.

3. A Basic Practise of Becoming Aware of the Breath

seated still and being aware that you are seated is the foundation of one of the earliest and most fundamental forms of meditation.

4. A Meditation on Compassion and Kindness

A meditation on loving-kindness designed to lessen the impact of unfavourable emotions such as worry and melancholy while increasing the impact of more favourable emotions such as pleasure and joy.

What are the benefits of practising mindfulness via meditation?

When we meditate, it is not helpful to concentrate on the advantages; rather, it is more helpful to merely perform the practise itself. Having said that, there are a significant number of advantages. Here are five reasons why you should start practising mindfulness now.

I am aware of your suffering. Although suffering is an inevitable part of life, you don't have to let it have power over you. You may transform your connection with both mental and physical suffering via the practise of mindfulness.

Improve your connections. Have you ever found yourself looking blankly at a friend, partner, or kid as they speak, with no idea what it is that they are saying? Practising mindfulness enables you to give them your undivided attention.

Reduce your tension. There is a growing body of research suggesting that prolonged exposure to high levels of stress may develop a variety of diseases and make existing conditions worse. Stress is reduced when one practises mindfulness.

Put some thought into it. When our thoughts wander away from what we're working on and we're tugged in six different directions, it may be annoying. Our natural capacity for concentration may be improved via meditation.

Cut down on Brilliant conversation. The voice in our heads that is always babbling and chatting away at us seems like it will never leave us alone.

WHY SHOULD ONE MAKE AN EFFORT TO BE MINDFUL?

Some of the most widely held misconceptions about mindfulness aren't even close to being accurate. When you first begin to put it into practise, you could also find that the journey is rather different from what you had anticipated. There is a very real possibility that you may end up being pleasantly pleased.

Barry Boyce, the editor-in-chief of Mindful, puts the record straight on these five misconceptions that people have about mindfulness:

Being mindful is not about "fixing" yourself in any way.

It is not necessary to silence your mind in order to practise mindfulness.

There is currently no religious affiliation associated with mindfulness.

The practise of mindfulness is no longer an escape from the world.

Achieve Mental Calmness While Maintaining Your Focus

If you have been dealing with issues such as anxiety, stress, or depression, the term "peace of mind" may seem like something out of a storybook to you at this point. Having said that, I can only guarantee you that there is such a thing as mental tranquilly in the actual world.

And now, in addition to that, it is something that you are capable of achieving in your own life.

It's a commonplace fallacy amongst people that tranquilly may best be attained in a state of living in which there aren't any stresses or strains to be dealt with; nonetheless, this isn't always the case. Finding mental peace and a focus point go hand in hand with one another. Therefore, you may achieve inner tranquilly by learning how to remain focused and gaining control over your thoughts. This will allow you to stop worrying about things. It is difficult to maintain peace of mind if you are unable to concentrate your attention. The more ingrained this pattern becomes in your life, the less challenging it will be to maintain a kingdom that is at peace at all times.

A General Explanation Of Meditation

Sitting quietly in a calm setting while maintaining a contemplative frame of mind is just one aspect of the practise of meditation. It requires forming connections, genuine ties to the things you do on a daily basis. Meditation is an age-old practise that consists of sitting in quiet reflection while focusing one's attention on a particular idea or object. When you engage in a practise like meditation, you'll find that it helps you see and comprehend things more clearly than you ever have before. When you meditate, you take stock of everything that is going on in your life and in you as a whole at the same time. You are going to realise that in the past, you had a difficult time comprehending yourself. However, with the assistance of meditation, you are able to learn more about yourself. It contributes to your personal growth and reveals to you a more positive outlook on life.

It is not true that in order to learn how to meditate, you need to be a religious person who practises religious rites. Although many religious traditions are components of meditation practises, this does not mean that in order to learn how to meditate, you need to be a religious person. You are free to begin at any point along your journey and to educate yourself independently.

You will be able to get a more profound understanding of who you are and who you have the potential to become by doing meditation. Your genuine personality and the areas of expertise in which you excel will become more apparent to you as time passes. When you meditate, you open up new pathways of awareness in both your heart and your intellect, which ultimately leads to a more satisfying existence. When you gain awareness, you begin to completely notice every event and milestone that is occurring in your life while it is happening. This allows you to truly appreciate the journey that you are on.

The following is a list of some additional advantages of meditation:

You may improve your knowledge of the mind and your ability to utilise it effectively via the practise of meditation. You are able to alleviate some of the tension and worry that is present in your life by practising meditation.

One of the purposes of meditation is to assist a person in better comprehending herself or herself. You are one of a kind in your own special manner, yet everyone else shares their humanity.

Your perspective will expand as you practise meditation. It motivates you to discover the resources inside yourself as well as your own unique creativity. When you meditate, you may experience feelings that drive you to squeeze as much value as possible out of each day.

Everyone wants their minds to be at peace, and if you meditate regularly, you'll find that you have more energy to devote to living a rich and fulfilling life. You will also find that your sleep is more rejuvenating and peaceful.

A person who meditates is able to make the most of any chance, no matter how seemingly little it may seem.

The body may become more relaxed via the practise of meditation. When a person is in a calm condition, it helps their whole body since it indicates that their heart rate and blood pressure are stable, that they have excellent posture, and that they have greater energy. When you meditate, the waves of your brain are in a different condition than when they are when you are walking or when you are sleeping. The mind and the body become one when one practises meditation. And most importantly, you may teach yourself to remove yourself from problematic and stressful ideas, which will allow you to improve your attention.

Various approaches to meditation for creative expression

So how exactly does one meditate? This will provide you with a few simple methods that you may experiment with as a starting point.

Technique 1 of Creative Meditation Is Known As "The Energy Booster"

The primary objective of this method is to leave you feeling calm yet at the same time energised. It's a wonderful one to do in the morning, or in the middle of the day if you encounter a break in energy about 3 o'clock in the afternoon.

It is possible to use this method while standing; however, some people find it more comfortable to sit on the edge of a chair with their spines aligned and both feet planted firmly on the ground.

To start, sit quietly with your eyes closed and focus on taking few deep breaths. Imagine that your whole body is breathing and that each and every cell is drawing in vitality from the surrounding air.

When you feel like you've got your bearings, bring your attention to your feet. They have a sense of the earth underneath them. Feel your feet connecting to the earth as you breathe in and out (it doesn't matter whether you aren't on the ground level or are seated indoors; just envision in your mind that your feet are connected to the earth).

Imagine that you are sucking up luscious, golden energy from the ground up via the bottoms of your feet as you take a deep breath in. Imagine it climbing your legs and entering your body quickly. Imagine that when you exhale, this golden light is permeating your whole body and seeping into each and every cell, supplying it with nutrients and giving it the vitality it needs.

Continue to imagine that you are exhaling the energy that you have absorbed from the soil into your cells as you continue to breathe it in via your feet. You may keep going for as long as you wish, but give it a go for at least 10 inhalations and exhalations.

When you feel as if you have accomplished everything that you set out to do, exhale completely and shut your eyes as you take a minute to focus on the energy that is there throughout your body. Open your eyes in a slow and gentle manner, and carry this sensation with you as you go about your day.

Technique 2 of Creative Meditation: "The Inventory Check"

This strategy is fairly straightforward, and it is an effective method for assessing how you are doing on a physical, mental, and emotional level right now. This is a useful strategy to use if you find that you are often pressed for time, under a lot of stress, or focused on things that are happening outside of yourself; it will assist you in returning to your body and refocusing your attention.

You should start in a seated posture, either on a cushion on the floor or sitting on the edge of a chair with a straight spine; whatever is most comfortable for you should be how you start.

Focus your focus on your breath and become aware of how it feels as it moves in and out of your body. Take note of the rise and fall of your chest as you inhale and exhale, as well as the gentle sensation of air passing over your top lip. If you find it difficult to maintain your focus on your breath, it may be beneficial to tell yourself mentally, "breathing in, breathing out," as you inhale and exhale. This might help you keep your attention on your breath.

Now, moving carefully from your feet upwards, begin to move your attention all the way through your actual body. Bring your focus to your feet, moving upward through your legs, hips, and torso, then down your arms to your hands, and then back up your arms, over your chest, and up to the crown of your head. Take note of any feelings that occur to you at this time. Make an effort not to pass judgement on these experiences; instead, pay attention to them and then let them pass.

Next, focus your attention to your heart, and pay attention to any feelings that you may be experiencing at this moment. It's possible that you'll experience pleasure, grief, stress, or even tranquilly. It's totally normal for you to feel numb or like nothing is happening; don't worry about it. Again, pay attention to what it is that you are experiencing without passing judgement, and then let the sensations to pass.

Finally, direct your focus inside to your mind and become aware of any ideas that occur to you at this time. You should make an effort to avoid being preoccupied with your thoughts; but, if this does happen, you should acknowledge that it has taken place and then return your attention to concentrating on your mind. You should make an effort to think of the ideas that come into your head as being analogous to the weather in your head; just observe what is there and let it pass without passing judgement.

After concentrating on your thoughts, return your attention back to your breathing and try to feel the air going into and out of your body with each inhale and exhale. Before opening your eyes and getting back to your day, take a moment to focus on your breathing and do it slowly and deeply for about a minute.

When You Are Under Pressure, What Can You Expect To Happen?

When a person is stressed, their heart rate speeds up, they become more tense in their muscles, they breathe more quickly, and the volume of blood that flows to their muscles and brain may rise by as much as 400%. When you are under a lot of stress on a consistent basis, not only is your physical health at risk, but so is your mental and emotional wellbeing.

When you're under a lot of pressure, your body reacts by giving you headaches, back pain, stomach difficulties, weariness, and a whole host of other symptoms that you're definitely going to be able to feel. Stress is causing numerous changes to take place behind the scenes, and these changes are also occuring. Stress may have an effect on the white blood cells in your body that help you fight infections. It can also raise the risk of stress and heart attacks, and it can lead to risky behaviours such as smoking, drug use, and alcohol use. Your sexual health may also be significantly impacted by stress. When you are under a lot of pressure, the thought of having sex is usually the last thing from your mind. The fact that it is more difficult to have an orgasm when you are stressed is another factor that adds to the pessimistic attitude on sexual encounters.

It is very necessary for you to figure out how to exercise control over the sources of stress in your life if you want to lead a lifestyle that is healthy and emotionally stable. You need to be able to recognise the signs of stress as they appear, and you also need to be able to acquire coping mechanisms that will assist you in feeling less overwhelmed.

How to Get Rid of Your Stress

If you are reading this book, you are either at the end of your rope with stress or you want to get right down to business and put an end to stress before it has a chance to interfere with your life. Getting rid of stress in your life may be accomplished in a variety of different methods, some of which we have already discussed. The most effective approach is often one that makes use of a number of these various techniques and approaches concurrently. On the other hand, you may also try meditating in order to put an end to the problem once and for all.

You should discuss the possibility of taking anti-anxiety medication with your primary care physician. These drugs may provide short-term relief from the symptoms of worry and stress. There is a wide variety of drugs available that may assist in the reduction or removal of stress. Medication is something that should only be taken for short-term periods of time, and it is not always the best option for every person. There is a possibility of becoming addicted to some anti-anxiety drugs, so this is something else that should be taken into account.

In addition to taking medication, you could also find that participating in psychotherapy might be of aid to you in working through the issues that are causing you to feel stressed. It is always comforting to have someone there with whom you can chat and who is willing to listen to what you are experiencing and how you are feeling. Talking to a therapist is beneficial for a number of reasons, one of which is the opportunity to get helpful guidance and pointers for managing stress. However, at the end of the day, there is only so much that can be accomplished for you by talking to another person. To alleviate the stress in your life, it is still up to you to take the required actions and get your life in order.

Meditation, on the other hand, is without a doubt the most effective strategy for removing stress from one's life. When you meditate, you are doing a lot more than merely momentarily restraining the tension that is buried deep within of you. You are removing it from your life, as well as your head and the ideas that you have. You are breaking free of your shackles. Meditation is completely safe to practise; there are no possible negative consequences, no fears, and no hazards linked with doing so. People who use meditation to alleviate stress discover that it not only helps them reduce the amount of stress they are now feeling but also helps them better manage and reduce the amount of stress they will experience in the future.

The practise of altering the way you think by gradually transitioning into a different mental state via the use of your thinking process is what is known as meditation. When you alter the way that you think, your whole mental state changes, and with that shift comes a rapid disappearance of stress and the symptoms associated with it.

Methods That Will Simplify Your Life And Help You Become More Satisfied

When you meditate often, you clear the mental clutter that's been building up inside of you, and as a result, your life becomes easier and less confusing. Increasing your sense of fulfilment may also be accomplished in the following ways:

You need to get rid of all the clutter if you want to live a simpler life. Although meditation helps you get rid of the congestion in your head, you also need to get rid of the clutter around you. Disorganisation is a fundamental contributor to feelings of tension and worry. Clearing the clutter from your life will also clear the clutter from your thinking.

Simplify your understanding of what it means to be successful. If you will only consider yourself to have achieved success until you have amassed a billion dollars, you will never be content. Make your idea of success more grounded in reality and less focused on acquiring material things.

You may better control your cravings and desires via meditation, which in turn makes it easier to stay within your financial limits. If you do not live within your means, you will accumulate debt, and this may be a source of a great deal of worry for you throughout your life. Do not put yourself in financial ruin in an effort to impress other people.

Learn to accept yourself and your life for who you are and what you have achieved via meditation, which helps you internalise the notion of "enough." You may also improve this ability by becoming more familiar with the meaning of the phrase "enough" Do not put undue pressure on yourself to acquire items that you do not genuinely need.

Forgiveness is facilitated through meditation, which also helps you become more receptive to being forgiven. It is necessary for you to release all of the resentment that you have inside your heart in order to make your life more fulfilling and less complex. Always keep in mind that the act of forgiving others will bring happiness and a sense of fulfilment to your life.

A life that is lived with an open mind is one that is filled with more intriguing and pleasurable experiences. Think on the perspectives and judgements of other people, since it's possible that they're correct.

Master the art of delegation, and resist the need to micromanage everything. Have faith that other people will take care of things for you. It will make things a great deal less difficult for you.

Simply putting on a happy face may make even the worst pain or tension disappear. Your life will become easier and more enjoyable once you realise you don't need to sweat the little stuff and simply smile.

Problems That Frequently Affect Children's Sleep

There are a lot of people who aren't aware of the reasons why certain kids have trouble falling or staying asleep. Many people feel that it is because kids have too much excess energy, don't want to go to sleep, or are just being tough with their parents on purpose. However, children may suffer a wide variety of difficulties falling asleep and staying asleep, which can result in the kid having trouble going to bed, remaining in bed, and waking up relaxed and happy.

The reasons why your kid is having trouble falling or staying asleep can change depending on how old they are. For instance, younger children, such as babies and newborns, are more prone to have sleep disruptions owing to indigestion, colic, or other physiological causes. These conditions may also cause other kinds of sleep problems. Young children are less likely to have difficulty falling or staying asleep due to night terrors or worry.

As your kid ages, goes through developmental milestones, and changes, the reasons why your child may have trouble falling or staying asleep will also vary and evolve with time.

According to the Sleep Foundation (n.d.), there are generally six different types of sleep difficulties that are the most frequent among youngsters.

Fears and phobias

The first difficulty sleeping that the vast majority of people, both children and adults, will encounter at least once in their lives is that of having nightmares.

Nightmares may be brought on by frightening thoughts or experiences, but sometimes they occur for no apparent reason at all. The majority of the time, they are brought on by stress. Believe it or not, this is the reason why youngsters may still have nightmares despite the fact that they are not exposed to any inherently disturbing pictures over the course of their day.

Nightmares might be one-time occurrences, or they can progress into recurring nightmares that take place night after night. Children are unable to come to the realisation that what they saw in their nightmare was not real, but adults are able to do so after being awoken from a bad dream. This allows adults to more easily go back asleep and have a comfortable night's sleep. It's possible that a youngster won't be able to tell the difference between a nightmare and the actual world, depending on their age as well as the specifics of the bad dream they had. As a result, the youngster is unable to go back asleep since their dreams keep them up. This is in addition to the fact that their sleep is first disrupted.

The conditions known as sleepwalking and sleep paralysis

Other forms of difficulty falling or staying asleep that are common in youngsters include sleepwalking and sleep paralysis. The phenomenon known as "sleepwalking" refers to when a person is sleeping yet is able to move about and even do complex tasks while in a dreamlike state. On the other hand, sleep paralysis occurs when a person wakes up and is no longer sleeping yet discovers that they are unable to move.

These terrifying sleep disruptions might result in devastating experiences for the person who experiences them when they wake up. One of the reasons of sleepwalking and sleep paralysis is excessive amounts of stress, but there are other factors that may contribute to these conditions as well. However, if you do not know what may trigger sleepwalking and sleep paralysis and if you do not put certain safeguards in place to keep the person safe, it may be rather difficult to deal with these sleep disruptions.

Snoring and Obstructive Sleep Apnea

Snoring and sleep apnea are two additional related sleep disorders that may prevent anybody, even children, from having a pleasant night's sleep. Both of these conditions are caused by the airway being blocked during sleep. Additionally, sleep apnea carries a risk of serious complications. Snoring may be brought on by a number of different factors, including the relaxation of the muscles in an individual's throat and tongue when they sleep, as well as allergies and viruses like the common cold. The recurring pausing and restarting of breathing over the course of the night is the hallmark symptom of sleep apnea.

Unfortunately, in most cases, the person experiencing either of these sleep disruptions is not aware that they exist until someone else who is awake witnesses them. The fact that children often sleep in their own rooms by themselves makes it more likely that their snoring and sleep apnea will go undiagnosed. Additionally, children tend to sleep more quietly than adults.

On the other hand, if one of these sleep disruptions is present, the person would most likely awaken feeling exhausted and with a disposition that suggests they are unhappy.

Syndrome of the Restless Legs

The phrase "restless leg syndrome" refers to the condition in which a person, even when they are at rest, cannot resist the need to move or shake their legs. The impulse to scratch might seem like an unpleasant and even excruciating itching that creeps up the leg. At this point, the only thing that will help is if the person shakes their legs or moves their legs about. As is the case with the vast majority of sleep disruptions, restless leg syndrome may be brought on by a wide variety of factors or occur for no apparent reason at all. Stress, on the other hand, is an element of life that is almost always present in the lives of those who have restless leg syndrome. In saying so, restless leg syndrome may be a harmless illness, or it can be a symptom that something more severe is going on in the body, such as pregnancy, an iron deficiency, or a chemical imbalance. In other words, the disease can be benign or it can be an indication of something more serious.

The vast majority of people, particularly adults, are able to articulate that they are experiencing pain and discomfort in their legs and have an understanding of the many techniques that might alleviate that pain. However, a correct diagnosis is far more difficult to arrive at when the condition is diagnosed in youngsters. In most cases, the condition known as restless leg syndrome is incorrectly classified as 'growing pains' or as cramps caused by dehydration. It's possible that children won't be able to comprehend the many coping tactics that are available to assist alleviate the pain associated with restless leg syndrome.

Discomfort in the Bodily Regions

Your kid may have problems falling or staying asleep for a variety of reasons, including general physical pain. It is also possible that this aspect contributes to some of the aforementioned difficulties with sleeping.

For example, the kid may have had an injury that prevents them from sleeping in the posture that they normally and like to sleep in, or that simply generally causes them to be uncomfortable and in pain. Either way, this makes it difficult for the child to get enough sleep. Internal discomfort is another kind of physical distress that a person may experience. This indicates that the youngster may be suffering from a condition such as indigestion, an upset stomach, or a headache, all of which might interfere with their normal sleep pattern.

Your kid may have trouble falling or staying asleep as a result of experiencing one or more uncomfortable bodily sensations, which may also have an adverse effect on the dreams that they have.

The strain

The last kind of difficulty falling or staying asleep is stress. This is a more generalised kind of sleep difficulty that children experience since it has the potential to contribute to, impact, and bring about any of the aforementioned forms of sleep disruption. Your kid may experience a buildup of stress, which may then present itself in a variety of ways. For instance, stress may result in a variety of bodily aches and pains, restless leg syndrome, and nightmares. Therefore, stress is one kind of broad and underlying difficulty sleeping, which is often associated to other forms of difficulty sleeping.

Because of this, if you take steps to reduce the amount of stress that your kid is exposed to in their daily life, you may in turn see favourable outcomes in the many different forms of sleep issues that may occur.

* * *

As can be seen, many of the challenges and difficulties that youngsters face are the same as those that adults face. It is essential to keep in mind that children and adults do not, in and of themselves, vary all that much from one another. In point of fact, kids are really little replicas of adults and are thus capable of experiencing the same or comparable challenges as adults. However, adults have a greater capacity than children do to comprehend and articulate the nature of the issue (Sleep Foundation, n.d.).

Children tend to have a more difficult time falling and staying asleep. Again, children often lack the capacity to comprehend that a nightmare is not based in reality, and they also frequently lack the verbal skills necessary to convey to their parents that their legs are uncomfortable and restless. However, the youngster may benefit from practising mindfulness in order to address both of these seeming shortcomings. In the end, it may be of assistance with the many difficulties that individuals may have falling or staying asleep.

An Explanation Of The Chakras

First things first, allow me to explain the concept of a chakra to you. The concept of the energy wheel is implied by the Sanskrit term chakra, which originates from that language. There are a variety of frequencies being vibrated by the energy that surrounds us. In point of fact, energy permeates the whole of the world, even in dimensions that our five senses are unable to detect (we refer to them as the spiritual realms). The life-giving energy that permeates the totality of everything that has ever been or ever will be may be found across the expanse of the cosmos. It is always present in the environment around us and circulates throughout the body.

What exactly are the Chakras?

A chakra is a location in the body where energy accumulates before continuing on its trip through the body in order for us to operate at optimum and healthy levels. Within the human body, there are several smaller chakras in addition to the seven main chakras. In this book, we will be concentrating on the main chakras since this has the most influence on one's ability to heal and overall sense of well-being.

It is possible for chakras to get blocked, and when this takes place, there is an interruption in the energy flow and distribution that normally occurs throughout the body. This may put a person at risk for developing a wide variety of diseases and other health problems. In addition, an unhealthy condition may develop if correct energy flows are not realised, which can lead to difficulties in the physical body, the mental and emotional body, and the spiritual body. As a result, restoring balance to the chakras may improve almost every area of a person's health.

It is also possible for the chakras to be out of whack. When the chakras are out of balance, some elements of our being may become hyperactive, which can lead to dysfunctional behaviours or bad health. As we shall see, the chakras give energy for various components of our being. When the chakras are out of balance, certain aspects of our being can become overactive.

There is a distinct energy frequency associated with each of the chakras. Light has the same effect as well. As a consequence of this, each of the chakras is correlated with a particular colour, which ranges from less energetic to more energetic. Red, orange, yellow, green, blue, indigo, and purple are the energetic vibrational colours, progressing from lower energy to the greatest energy. Red is the lowest energy vibrational colour. There is no way that it could be a coincidence that they are also the colours of the rainbow.

In addition to this, an element and a particular region in the body are connected to each chakra. Chakras are not energy in and of themselves but rather are focal points where energy may be found. This energy flows freely and unobstructed through the body, mind, and soul of a healthy human, as well as the rest of the universe, resulting in a healthy equilibrium for the individual and the universe as a whole. When each of your chakras is functioning properly and is in perfect tune with the others, you will experience feelings of harmony, serenity, and satisfaction.

The first, or root, chakra

The root chakra is the foundational energy centre of the chakra system. It "roots" you to Mother Earth and offers you essential footing by connecting you to her. It is linked to feelings of safety and security, as well as the capacity to meet one's fundamental requirements, such as securing enough supplies of food, drink, and a roof over one's head. There is a strong connection between the root chakra and the experience of feeling comfortable and secure in one's environment. The base of the spine is the site of the root chakra, and the colour red is connected with this particular chakra. This is a reflection of the fact that the root chakra has the lowest vibrational frequency of the seven primary chakras.

The region of the sacral chakra

The sacral chakra is located in the area immediately above the root chakra. It is connected to your sexuality, your capacity to experience pleasure, as well as your creative potential. Due to the fact that it is involved with more advanced aspects of your existence, its vibrational frequency is greater than that of the root chakra. If a person is unable to meet the most basic demands for their safety, such as being able to get food and water, they are not going to be in a state that is conducive to feelings of joy and creativity. The sacral chakra may be found in the area just below the navel.

www.ingramcontent.com/pod-product-compliance
Lightning Source LLC
Chambersburg PA
CBHW050419120526
44590CB00015B/2026